LOCKED IN:

LIVING WITH FAITH IN A SHAKEN WORLD

A 52-Week Teen Devotional

DR. ELSWORTH NEALE

DEDICATION

To my daughter, *Juda*,

S haring a birthday with you is one of *God's sweetest gifts* to me. As you grow, step into your teenage years and beyond, my prayer is that your life will always stay anchored in *Christ*, no matter how shaken the world around you becomes.

To every teenager who feels like the world is shifting beneath their feet, this devotional is also for you. May each page remind you that you are not alone, that your faith matters deeply, and that *God has a unique plan and purpose for your life.* May you discover that *God's Word is the one foundation that never shakes,* and that your life, when rooted in *Him,* can shine brightly in any storm.

Juda, you inspired this work, but you are joined by countless young people who are learning, just like you, what it means to be *locked into faith.*

With love,

Dr. Elsworth Neale

INTRODUCTION

◄◆○◆►

L ife as a teen is complicated. Between school, family, friends, and the constant buzz of social media, it's easy to feel pulled in many different directions. Questions about *who you are, where you fit in,* and *what your future holds* can sometimes feel overwhelming.

This devotional was written for moments like that. It's here to remind you that your faith doesn't have to be fragile. God has called you to live *strong, steady,* and *locked in* on Him, even when everything around you feels uncertain.

Here's how to use this book:

- Read one devotional each week, then sit with it daily. Let the questions and prayer guide your journaling and actions throughout the week.

- Be honest with yourself as you reflect. God can handle your *questions, doubts,* and *struggles.*

- Look for ways to live out what you read. Faith isn't just about what you *know;* it's about how you *show* it.

This is not about *perfection.* It's about *progress.* As you walk with God day by day, you'll find your faith growing deeper, your choices becoming clearer, and your life bearing fruit that lasts.

Stay steady. Stay faithful. Stay locked in.

CONTENTS

THE APPLE: SWEETNESS THAT LASTS

WEEK 1:
BRUISED BUT SWEET

———◆○◆———

Hold up an apple. It looks shiny, but sometimes there is a bruise. At first glance, you might think it is ruined, but one bite proves the inside is still sweet. Life is like that. People see your bruises, the mistakes, the awkward moments, and the times when you didn't fit in. Maybe you see them too, every time you scroll, compare, or replay old words in your head. But bruises do not erase the sweetness God has placed inside you.

"Children are a gift from the Lord." (Psalm 127:3) That is you. Not flawless. Not fake- perfect. But chosen, loved, and full of God's sweetness.

Double-meaning phrase: *Bruised but sweet.*

Journal prompt: What is one "bruise" you carry? How could God turn it into a story of sweetness?

_____

_____

_____

_____

_____

_____

Prayer: God, thank you that even with bruises, you have placed sweetness within me. Help me live so that others taste Your kindness. Amen.

WEEK 2:
MIRROR CHECK

———◄◆O◆►———

When you look in the mirror, what do you notice first? The bruise or the beauty? The flaw or the gift? Most teens focus on the bruise. But God says something different. He calls you *His masterpiece.* He already sees the sweetness in you, even when you do not.

Imagine if you asked three close friends to describe you. Would they only point out the flaws, or would they see the moments when your sweetness shines? Often, others notice God's work in us more than we do.

"I praise You because I am fearfully and wonderfully made." (Psalm 139:14) You were made *on purpose, for purpose.*

Double-meaning phrase: *The bruise does not erase the beauty.*

Journal prompt: Write three things about yourself that are evidence of God's design.

_____

_____

_____

_____

_____

_____

> *Prayer: God, change my focus so I see myself the*
> *way You see me. Amen.*

WEEK 3:
CAFETERIA CHOICES

P icture this: someone in your school drops their tray. Food goes everywhere. Most of the room laughs.

What do you do? Choices like these reveal what is inside. Anyone can join the laughter, but sweetness shines when you choose compassion.

An outside observer once said about a student, *"You are the one who makes people feel welcome here."* That student was not perfect; they had their bruises. But what people remembered was their sweetness in small, daily choices.

"Let your light shine before others, that they may see your good deeds and glorify your Father in heaven." (Matthew 5:16)

Double-meaning phrase: *Your sweetness is louder than your bruise.*

Journal prompt: Think of one way you can shine sweetness this week at school. Then do it.

Prayer: Jesus, give me courage to choose kindness when it is easier to blend in with the crowd. Amen.

WEEK 4:
BITE INTO TRUTH

◆—◇—◆

When you finally bite into an apple, you discover what is inside. In the same way, when life tests you, what comes out shows what is really in your heart. Is it bitterness or sweetness?

God's Word is the truth that reminds you who you are. His Word keeps you sweet, even when life tries to sour you. Take time to *bite into the truth* every day. Just like fruit keeps your body healthy, God's Word keeps your spirit strong.

"Your words were found, and I ate them, and your words became to me a joy and the delight of my heart." (Jeremiah 15:16)

Double-meaning phrase: *Bite into truth, it keeps you sweet.*

Journal prompt: Read Psalm 34:8. Write about what it means to *"taste and see that the Lord is good."*

_____

_____

_____

_____

_____

_____

_____

> *Prayer: God, fill me with Your Word so that my life may reflect Your sweetness. Amen.*

THE MANGO:
POTENTIAL TAKES TIME

WEEK 5:
NOT YET DOESN'T
MEAN NOT EVER

———◆◇◆———

A mango starts out green, hard, and sour. Nobody wants to bite it then. But give it time, and it turns golden and sweet. Your life feels like that sometimes. You may not see your gifts fully grown yet, but that does not mean they are not real. It just means the season is not here yet.

A coach once told an athlete, *"You have what it takes, you just need time to grow into it."* You may not be first chair in band, the top scorer, or the most popular, but God already sees your golden stage.

"I know the plans I have for you," declares the Lord. (Jeremiah 29:11) His plan takes time.

Double-meaning phrase: *Not yet does not mean not ever.*

Journal prompt: Where do you feel behind? Ask God to help you wait with hope.

_____

_____

_____

_____

_____

Prayer: Lord, help me trust Your timing
for my life. Amen.

WEEK 6:
SEEDS OF DREAMS

———◆◇◆———

Inside every mango, there are seeds. They may look small, but they hold the future of many more trees and fruits. God has planted seeds of purpose in you, ideas, passions, and talents. They may feel small now, but they carry considerable potential.

A teacher once told a student, *"I see leadership in you."* The student laughed it off, but later those words pushed them to step up. Sometimes other people see seeds in you before you do.

"Though your beginning was small, your latter days will be very great." (Job 8:7)

Double-meaning phrase: *Small seeds, big future.*

Journal prompt: Write down one dream or gift you think God planted in you.

_____

_____

_____

_____

_____

_____

_____

> *Prayer: God, help me notice the seeds You have placed in me and trust them to grow. Amen.*

WEEK 7:
WHEN OTHERS DON'T SEE IT

S ome people look at a green mango and say, *"It is no good."* They judge too early. People may look at you now and not see the greatness God planted. That does not mean it is not there.

I once overheard a parent tell their teen, *"I do not get why you are wasting time on art."* But that teen kept drawing. Years later, their art spoke to hundreds of people. People will not always believe in your mango, but God does.

"Do not let anyone look down on you because you are young, but set an example..." (1 Timothy 4:12)

Double-meaning phrase: *They may not see it, but God does.*

Journal prompt: Have you ever been overlooked? Write how God sees you differently.

_____

_____

_____

_____

_____

> *Prayer: Lord, give me the strength to persevere when others do not recognize my gifts. Help me stay faithful. Amen.*

WEEK 8:
GOLDEN IN SEASON

———◆◇◆———

When the mango ripens, it is unmistakable, golden, fragrant, and ready. That is how it feels when your gifts start to shine. It is not overnight. It is a season God prepares. And when it comes, your fruit blesses others.

Imagine trying to force a mango to ripen faster by squeezing it. You would only ruin it. Forcing your gifts out of season leaves you frustrated, but when you wait, your season will be sweet.

"At the proper time we will reap a harvest if we do not give up." (Galatians 6:9)

Double-meaning phrase: *Golden comes in season.*

Journal prompt: What is one area where you feel ready to give up? Ask God to help you stay patient.

_____

_____

_____

_____

_____

_____

_____

_____

_____

Prayer: God, teach me to wait for my golden season. Amen.

THE BANANA:
STRENGTH IN COMMUNITY

WEEK 9:
WE GROW IN CLUSTERS

———◆◇◆———

Bananas do not grow alone; they hang together in bunches. That is God's design for you, too. You were not meant to do life solo. You need people—friends, mentors, and your church—to help you grow and develop.

One student once told me, *"I thought I had to figure out faith by myself, but then I joined youth group and realized I wasn't alone."* Growth happens in a community.

"And let us consider how we may spur one another on toward love and good deeds." (Hebrews 10:24)

Double-meaning phrase: *Faith ripens best in clusters.*

Journal prompt: Who are the people helping your faith ripen right now?

_____

_____

_____

_____

_____

_____

_____

_____

_____

> *Prayer: Lord, thank You for placing people around me.
> Help me lean on them and grow together.*

WEEK 10:
HOLDING EACH OTHER UP

W hen a banana cluster is heavy, the bananas support each other. In the same way, you need others to hold you up when life weighs you down.

A friend once said, *"You don't have to carry this alone."* Those words made all the difference. Sometimes God uses people to be the support you need.

"Two are better than one. If either of them falls down, one can help the other up." (Ecclesiastes 4:9–10)

Double-meaning phrase: *We hold each other up.*

Journal prompt: Write about a time when someone lifted you. How can you do the same for someone else this week?

_____

_____

_____

_____

_____

_____

_____

_____

Prayer: God, make me the kind of friend who holds others up when they are weak.

WEEK 11:
SHARING THE BUNCH

————◆◇◆————

A banana bunch has enough for everyone. That is how your gifts work—they are not just for you. God gave them so others could be blessed too.

Think about snacks at lunch. Do you keep them hidden, or do you share? Your talents, your time, your smile—they are all part of your "bunch."

"Each of you should use whatever gift you have received to serve others." (1 Peter 4:10)

Double-meaning phrase: *Bananas are better when shared.*

Journal prompt: What is one gift you can share with someone this week?

_____

_____

_____

_____

_____

_____

_____

_____

_____

_____

*Prayer: Lord, help me share what You have given me
instead of keeping it all to myself.*

WEEK 12:
GOD'S FAMILY

T he banana cluster only makes sense when it is part of the tree. In the same way, your smaller circle—friends, family, youth group—is part of something bigger: the family of God.

I once heard a leader say, *"The church is messy, but it is still family."* That is the truth. Families have struggles, but they also provide support, identity, and a sense of belonging.

"So, in Christ we, though many, form one body, and each member belongs to all the others." (Romans 12:5)

Double-meaning phrase: *You belong to the bunch.*

Journal prompt: How does being part of God's family make you feel less alone?

_____

_____

_____

_____

_____

_____

*Prayer: Father, thank You that I belong in Your family.
Help me value my church and the people You have placed
around me.*

THE GRAPE: STAYING CONNECTED

WEEK 13:
CONNECTED TO THE VINE

———◆○◆———

A grape cannot survive if it is cut off from the Vine. It shrivels up fast. That is how life works when we try to do it without Jesus. Staying connected to Him is the only way to remain spiritually alive.

I once heard a teen say, *"When I stop praying or reading my Bible, I feel dry."* That is exactly what happens—disconnected grapes do not thrive.

Jesus said, "I am the vine; you are the branches. If you remain in me and I in you, you will bear much fruit." (John 15:5)

Double-meaning phrase: *Stay plugged into the Vine.*

Journal prompt: What is one way you can reconnect with Jesus this week?

_____

_____

_____

_____

_____

_____

_____

_____

_____

_____

> *Prayer: Lord, help me stay connected to You so that my life may continue to bear fruit.*

WEEK 14:
FRUIT IN CLUSTERS

———◆◇◆———

Grapes do not grow one by one. They grow in clusters, side by side. Faith is not just *me and God*; it is *me, God, and the people He has placed around me.*

An outside observer once told a youth group, *"I can tell you guys actually love each other."*

That love spoke louder than any sermon.

"By this everyone will know that you are my disciples, if you love one another." (John 13:35)

Double-meaning phrase: *Faith shows best in clusters.*

Journal prompt: Who is in your "faith cluster"? Write their names and thank God for them.

_____

_____

_____

_____

_____

_____

_____

_____

_____

_____

Prayer: God, help me love my friends in Christ so others see You in us.

WEEK 15:
PRUNED FOR GROWTH

A gardener cuts back grapevines to encourage better fruit growth. Pruning looks harsh, but it is for the Vine's good. In your life, God may cut away habits, relationships, or attitudes that hold you back.

It can hurt when something is removed. But pruning is not punishment; it is preparation.

"Every branch that does bear fruit He prunes so that it will be even more fruitful." (John 15:2)

Double-meaning phrase: *Pruned but not punished.*

Journal prompt: What is something God might be cutting away in your life right now?

_____

_____

_____

_____

_____

_____

_____

> *Prayer: Father, help me trust Your pruning. I want to grow stronger fruit in You.*

WEEK 16:
PRESSED INTO PURPOSE

❖

Grapes are not just eaten—they are pressed into juice. Crushing may seem like the end, but it often brings out something new and valuable. Hard seasons in your life might feel like pressure, but God can use them to pour out blessings.

I once heard a teen say, *"That tough season made me stronger and gave me compassion for others."* That is the juice—what comes out when grapes are pressed.

"We are hard pressed on every side, but not crushed, struck down, but not destroyed." (2 Corinthians 4:8 9)

Double-meaning phrase: *Pressed but still with purpose.*

Journal prompt: Write about a time you felt pressured. How could God be using that season to bring something new out of you?

> *Prayer: God, when life presses me, let what comes out*
> *bring life to others.*

THE WATERMELON:
HIDDEN DEPTHS

WEEK 17:
DON'T JUDGE THE RIND

———◆◇◆———

On the outside, a watermelon appears tough, with a thick green rind that is heavy and unappealing. But cut it open, and the inside is bright, juicy, and sweet. People can be like that. You cannot always see what is inside by looking at the outside.

I once overheard someone say about a quiet student, *"They do not talk much, but when they do, it is deep."* That is watermelon truth—what is inside matters most.

"The Lord does not look at the things people look at. People look at the outward appearance, but the Lord looks at the heart." (1 Samuel 16:7)

Double-meaning phrase: *The rind isn't the real story.*

Journal prompt: Where in your life are you tempted to judge by appearances?

_____

_____

_____

_____

_____

_____

_____

> *Prayer: God, help me see myself and others the way You do, past the rind, straight to the heart.*

WEEK 18:
SEEDS INSIDE

E very watermelon slice has seeds. Some spit them out, but the truth is, seeds carry the future of more watermelons. In your life, God has placed seeds—talents, dreams, and opportunities that can multiply far beyond you.

A youth leader once said, *"Don't underestimate what God can plant through you."* You may feel small, but your seeds can grow big in His hands.

"Do not despise these small beginnings, for the Lord rejoices to see the work begin." (Zechariah 4:10)

Double-meaning phrase: *Seeds today, harvest tomorrow.*

Journal prompt: What is one small gift or idea God has planted in you? How could it multiply if you trusted Him with it?

_____

_____

_____

_____

_____

_____

_____

_____

> *Prayer: Lord, thank You for the seeds You have planted in me. Help me grow them faithfully.*

WEEK 19:
JOY OVERFLOWING

———◆◇◆———

C ut open a watermelon on a hot day, and everyone wants a piece. It is refreshing, joyful, and perfect for sharing. That is what God's joy in you is like—not meant to stay bottled up, but to overflow into others.

I once heard a student described as *"the kind of person whose laughter makes the whole room brighter."* That is watermelon joy—contagious and refreshing.

"The joy of the Lord is your strength." (Nehemiah 8:10)

Double-meaning phrase: *Joy that refreshes.*

Journal prompt: How can you share God's joy with someone who needs it this week?

_____

_____

_____

_____

_____

_____

_____

_____

> *Prayer: God, fill me with joy so strong that it overflows into the people around me.*

WEEK 20:
MESSY BUT WORTH IT

E ating watermelon is not neat. Juice runs down your hands and chin, seeds scatter everywhere, and sometimes it gets sticky. But the mess is worth it for the sweetness. Faith is like that. Following Jesus will not always be neat or easy, but it is always worth it.

A teen once admitted, *"Living for God makes me stand out. It is messy sometimes, but I would not trade it."* That is watermelon faith—a little messy, but full of life.

"Whoever wants to be my disciple must deny themselves and take up their cross and follow me." (Matthew 16:24)

Double-meaning phrase: *Messy faith is still genuine faith.*

Journal prompt: What is one messy part of your faith journey right now? How is God showing you it is still worth it?

_____

_____

_____

_____

_____

_____

Prayer: Lord, thank You that even when following You
feels messy, it is worth every step.

THE CHERRY:
SMALL BUT PRECIOUS

WEEK 21:
TINY BUT POWERFUL

C herries are small compared to other fruits, but they pack amazing flavor and nutrition. You might feel small—your voice overlooked, your presence unnoticed—but God does not measure impact by size. Even small actions can have a significant impact on someone's entire day.

A teacher once told a shy student, *"Your quiet kindness speaks louder than words."* Tiny, but powerful.

"Do not despise these small beginnings, for the Lord rejoices to see the work begin." (Zechariah 4:10)

Double-meaning phrase: *Small doesn't mean insignificant.*

Journal prompt: What is one "small" thing you have done that actually made a difference?

_____

_____

_____

_____

_____

_____

*Prayer: God, thank You that You use even the
little things in significant ways.*

WEEK 22:
DOUBLE FRUIT

———◆◇◆———

Cherries often grow in pairs, two hanging side by side. That is a reminder of the power of partnership. God did not design you to do life alone—you grow stronger with others.

I once heard a friend tell another, *"I would not have made it through without you."* That is the cherry truth—life is sweeter when shared.

"Two are better than one, because they have a good return for their labor." *(Ecclesiastes 4:9)*

Double-meaning phrase: *Faith grows better in twos.*

Journal prompt: Who is the "cherry partner" in your life? How can you thank them this week?

_____

_____

_____

_____

_____

_____

_____

_____

_____

> *Prayer: Lord, thank You for the people You have placed beside me. Help me be a faithful friend in return.*

WEEK 23:
DON'T UNDERESTIMATE YOURSELF

———◆◇◆———

Because cherries are so small, people can forget how good they are. Maybe you feel that way too—underestimated or overlooked. But God sees your worth, even when others do not.

A youth leader once said, *"The quietest student in this room might have the deepest faith."*

Do not let size fool you.

"The Lord is my strength and my shield. My heart leaps for joy, and with my song I praise Him." (Psalm 28:7)

Double-meaning phrase: *Overlooked doesn't mean unimportant.*

Journal prompt: Write about a time you felt underestimated. How might God have been shaping you in that moment?

_____

_____

_____

_____

_____

> *Prayer: God, remind me that even when others underestimate me, You never do.*

WEEK 24:
SWEET IMPACT

—◆◇◆—

A single cherry can top a dessert, adding sweetness to it. Small but memorable. That is your life when you follow Christ—you leave a sweet impact, even if it seems small at the time.

One student told me, *"I thought my encouragement did not matter, but later someone said it kept them from giving up."* That is cherry power.

"Let your conversation be always full of grace, seasoned with salt, so that you may know how to answer everyone." (Colossians 4:6)

Double-meaning phrase: *Little fruit, lasting flavor.*

Journal prompt: Who could you encourage this week with a few simple words?

_____

_____

_____

_____

_____

_____

_____

_____

_____

Prayer: Lord, make my words and actions sweet to those around me. Amen.

THE PINEAPPLE

STRENGTH WITH SWEETNESS

WEEK 25:
SPIKY OUTSIDE, SWEET INSIDE

———◆———

A pineapple's outside is rough, spiky, and uninviting. But once you cut it open, the inside is golden and sweet. Some people put up a tough exterior because they have been hurt or do not want to look weak. Maybe you do too. But God calls us to let the sweetness He placed in us show, even if we have had to be tough on the outside.

I once heard someone say about a friend, *"He looks intimidating, but he is the kindest person I know."* Do not let the spikes fool you.

"Man looks at the outward appearance, but the Lord looks at the heart." (1 Samuel 16:7)

Double-meaning phrase: *Strong outside, sweet inside.*

Journal prompt: Do you ever hide behind a "spiky" exterior? What sweetness could you show instead?

_____

_____

_____

_____

_____

_____

> *Prayer: God, soften my heart so Your sweetness*
> *can shine through me.*

WEEK 26:
WEAR YOUR CROWN

———◆◇◆———

The pineapple wears a crown—a reminder of dignity and confidence. You do not have to walk with your head down, even when life gets tough. You are chosen, royal, and valuable in God's eyes.

I once heard a youth leader tell a student, *"You do not even realize how much confidence you carry—others look up to you."* That is the crown you already wear.

"You are a chosen people, a royal priesthood, a holy nation, God's special possession." (1 Peter 2:9)

Double-meaning phrase: *Wear your crown with confidence.*

Journal prompt: What is one way you can walk with more confidence in who God made you to be?

_____

_____

_____

_____

_____

_____

_____

> *Prayer: Lord, help me remember I am chosen*
> *and crowned by You.*

WEEK 27:
PROTECT WHAT MATTERS

◆◇◆

The pineapple's spiky armor protects what is valuable inside. In the same way, God calls you to guard your heart and faith. That does not mean shutting people out—it means being careful what you let in.

A mentor once said, *"Not everything deserves a place in your heart."* That is wisdom. *"Above all else, guard your heart, for everything you do flows from it."* (Proverbs 4:23) **Double-meaning phrase:** *Guard the sweetness.*

Journal prompt: What is one boundary you need to set to protect your heart?

_____

_____

_____

_____

_____

_____

_____

_____

_____

Prayer: God, give me wisdom to guard my heart without closing it off.

WEEK 28:
HOSPITALITY FRUIT

———◆◇◆———

Pineapples are a symbol of hospitality. They welcome people in, reminding us that strength and sweetness go hand in hand with generosity.

I once heard a teen described as *"the one who makes everyone feel included."* That is pineapple hospitality.

"Do not forget to show hospitality to strangers, for by so doing some people have shown hospitality to angels without knowing it." (Hebrews 13:2)

Double-meaning phrase: *Strong enough to welcome.*

Journal prompt: Who could you welcome or include this week?

_____

_____

_____

_____

_____

_____

_____

_____

_____

_____

> *Prayer: Lord, make me strong enough to be kind, and*
> *kind enough to be welcoming.*

THE ORANGE
WHOLENESS IN CHRIST

WEEK 29:
ONE FRUIT, MANY SLICES

An orange is one fruit, but when you peel it open, you see many slices. That's like you — one person with many sides: talents, emotions, thoughts, and dreams. God created every part of you with purpose, and all the slices make you who you are.

A teacher once told a student, *"Don't hide the parts of you that are different — they're all part of what makes you whole."*

"For you created my inmost being; you knit me together in my mother's womb." (Psalm 139:13)

Double-meaning phrase: *Every slice matters.*

Journal prompt: What's one "slice" of who you are that you sometimes ignore? How can you honor it this week?

_____

_____

_____

_____

_____

_____

_____

_____

> *Prayer: God, thank You for making me whole,*
> *piece by piece.*

WEEK 30:
SHARED LIFE

———◆◇◆———

Oranges are easy to share. You peel one open, and suddenly everyone has a slice. That's what a Christian community is supposed to look like — sharing life.

I once heard someone say about their youth group, *"It feels like family because no one goes without."* That's orange life.

"All the believers were together and had everything in common... They broke bread in their homes and ate together with glad and sincere hearts." (Acts 2:44, 46)

Double-meaning phrase: *Life is sweeter when it's shared.*

Journal prompt: Who can you share life with this week — your time, encouragement, or help?

_____

_____

_____

_____

_____

_____

_____

_____

> ***Prayer:*** *Lord, help me live open-handed and*
> *share my life with others.*

WEEK 31:
UNITY IN DIVERSITY

No two orange slices are the same size, but they all belong to the same fruit. In the same way, you and your friends may be very different — different talents, backgrounds, and personalities. But in Christ, you belong together.

A youth leader once told their group, *"Our differences aren't problems — they're proof of God's creativity."*

"Just as a body, though one, has many parts... so it is with Christ." (1 Corinthians 12:12)

Double-meaning phrase: *Different slices, one fruit.*

Journal prompt: How can you celebrate someone's differences instead of competing with them?

Prayer: God, thank You for diversity in the body of Christ. Teach me to value every part.

WEEK 32:
COMPLETE IN CHRIST

W hen the orange is whole, it's complete. In the same way, you'll never feel whole without Christ at the center. You may try to fill the gaps with friends, success, or likes online, but true wholeness comes from Him alone.

A student once admitted, *"I kept trying to fit in, but I only felt whole when I realized my identity is in Jesus."*

"So, you also are complete through your union with Christ." (Colossians 2:10, NLT)

Double-meaning phrase: *Only Christ makes me whole.*

Journal prompt: Where do you look for completeness outside of Christ? Write one way to shift your focus back to Him.

Prayer: Jesus, be the center that makes me whole.

THE STRAWBERRY: GROWING LOW & HUMBLE

WEEK 33:
CLOSE TO THE GROUND

◄─◆◄●►◆─►

Strawberries don't grow tall like trees. They spread low, close to the earth. That's humility — not needing to be the highest or loudest to have value. Jesus lived this way. Even though He was God, He humbled Himself to serve others.

I once heard a teacher describe a student as *"quiet, but the glue that holds the group together."* That's strawberry strength — humble but powerful.

"Humble yourselves before the Lord, and he will lift you." (James 4:10)

Double-meaning phrase: *Greatness grows low.*

Journal prompt: Where in your life do you need to choose humility instead of pride?

---

*Prayer: God, teach me to grow low so I can
reflect Your greatness.*

WEEK 34:
SPREADING RUNNERS

S trawberry plants grow by sending out "runners" that spread and root into new places. That's how influence works — small acts of faith spread further than you realize.

A youth leader once said, *"Your faith is like ripples in water — you don't always see how far they go."* Every prayer, every act of kindness, every quiet *yes* to God sends out a runner.

"Let us not become weary in doing good, for at the proper time we will reap a harvest." (Galatians 6:9)

Double-meaning phrase: *Faith spreads like runners.*

Journal prompt: What's one act of faith you can "plant" this week to influence others?

_____

_____

_____

_____

_____

_____

_____

_____

> *Prayer: Lord, help my small acts of faith*
> *spread further than I can see.*

WEEK 35:
SWEET AT THE BOTTOM

Strawberries grow low to the ground, but that's where their sweetness forms. In the same way, serving from the low place produces the sweetest results.

I once overheard someone say about a teen, *"They're always willing to help, even when no one notices."* That's strawberry sweetness — humble service that blesses everyone around.

"The greatest among you will be your servant." (Matthew 23:11)

Double-meaning phrase: *Sweetness grows in low places.*

Journal prompt: What's one "low" way you can serve someone this week?

_____

_____

_____

_____

_____

_____

_____

_____

_____

_____

_____

> **Prayer:** *God, help me find sweetness in serving others quietly.*

WEEK 36:
HARVESTED TOGETHER

———◆◇◆———

Strawberries are rarely picked one at a time. They're gathered together, basket after basket. That's how God designed the church, too — not lone faith, but shared faith. We grow low, and we're harvested together.

A farmer once said about strawberries, *"The joy is in the gathering."* That's the joy of community — we don't walk this road alone.

"Now you are the body of Christ, and each one of you is a part of it." (1 Corinthians 12:27)

Double-meaning phrase: *We grow low, we rise together.*

Journal prompt: Who's in your "basket" of faith? Thank God for them and pray for them this week.

Prayer: Lord, thank You that I don't grow alone. Teach me to value community in Your harvest.

THE COCONUT: LAYERS OF DISCOVERY

WEEK 37:
TOUGH OUTSIDE, TREASURE INSIDE

❖

A coconut looks rough, hairy, and hard to crack. But inside, there's refreshing water and nourishing meat. People are like that, too. Sometimes we put on a tough exterior so no one sees our struggles. But God knows the treasure inside.

A mentor once said, *"That student may look closed off, but once you get to know them, they're amazing."* Don't be fooled by the shell — the real value is inside.

"But the Lord said to Samuel, 'Do not consider his appearance or his height... the Lord looks at the heart.'" (1 Samuel 16:7)

Double-meaning phrase: *The shell isn't the whole story.*

Journal prompt: Do you ever hide behind a "hard shell"? What's one way you can let God or others see the real you?

_____

_____

_____

_____

_____

_____

> *Prayer: Lord, help me trust You with my inner being, not just my outer appearance.*

WEEK 38:
LIVING WATER

◄──◆◇◆──►

Crack open a coconut and you'll find refreshing water inside. God's Spirit is like that — living water for your soul. When you feel drained, He refreshes you from the inside out.

I once heard a teen say after youth camp, *"It felt like God filled me back up."* That's what the Spirit does — living water that revives your soul.

"Whoever believes in me, as Scripture has said, rivers of living water will flow from within them." (John 7:38)

Double-meaning phrase: *Living water flows within.*

Journal prompt: When was the last time you felt spiritually refreshed? Write what filled you up.

_____

_____

_____

_____

_____

_____

_____

_____

_____

> *Prayer: Holy Spirit, refresh me with Your*
> *living water today.*

WEEK 39:
NOURISHING OTHERS

———◄●○●►———

The white coconut meat is rich and nourishing. It strengthens and sustains. In the same way, your words and actions can nourish others — giving them encouragement, strength, and hope.

A teacher once said, *"Your encouragement is like food for the soul."* That's coconut truth — your life can feed others.

"Therefore encourage one another and build each other up." (1 Thessalonians 5:11)

Double-meaning phrase: *Be soul food for others.*

Journal prompt: Who in your life needs encouragement this week? Write one thing you could say or do for them.

_____

_____

_____

_____

_____

_____

_____

_____

_____

_____

Prayer: Lord, use me to nourish and strengthen the people around me.

WEEK 40:
WHOLE AND COMPLETE

———◆◇◆———

A coconut has layers — husk, shell, water, and meat. Each layer matters, but together they make the whole. You are the same: body, mind, Spirit, and soul. God made every part of you, and He cares about all of it.

A counselor once told a teen, *"Don't just care for your body — care for your soul too."*

Wholeness means letting God shape every layer.

"I praise you because I am fearfully and wonderfully made." (Psalm 139:14)

Double-meaning phrase: *Every layer matters to God.*

Journal prompt: Which "layer" of your life (body, mind, Spirit, soul) needs God's care most right now?

_____

_____

_____

_____

_____

_____

_____

_____

> *Prayer: Father, thank You for making me whole. Help me care for every layer of who I am.*

THE LEMON: RESILIENCE IN SOUR SEASONS

WEEK 41:
SOUR BUT ESSENTIAL

———◆◇◆———

Bite into a lemon by itself, and your whole face puckers. It's sour. But without lemons, so many foods would be flat. Life has sour seasons too — moments that sting, disappoint, or weigh heavily. They don't feel good, but they're essential for shaping who you are.

A teen once admitted, *"I hated going through that tough year, but now I see how much stronger I am."* Sour, but essential.

"Consider it pure joy, my brothers and sisters, whenever you face trials of many kinds." —James 1:2

Double-meaning phrase: *The sour seasons shape me.*

Journal prompt: What's a "sour" season you've faced? What did you learn from it?

_____

_____

_____

_____

_____

_____

_____

_____

Prayer: Lord, help me see how even the most difficult times grow my faith.

WEEK 42:
CLEAN AND HEAL

—◄◆○◆►—

Lemons don't just taste sour; they clean and heal. People use lemon to cleanse water, heal sore throats, or brighten what's dull. In the same way, trials purify your heart. They strip away what doesn't belong and make room for something fresh.

A mentor once told a student, *"God used that challenge to clean out bitterness and replace it with faith."* Sour, but healing.

"He will sit as a refiner and purifier of silver." — *Malachi 3:3*

Double-meaning phrase: *Sourness can heal.*

Journal prompt: Is there something God is cleaning out of your heart right now?

_____

_____

_____

_____

_____

_____

_____

_____

_____

*Prayer: God, use challenges to heal me and make
me more like You.*

WEEK 43:
LEMONADE MOMENTS

———◆◇◆———

People say, *"When life gives you lemons, make lemonade."* It's cliché, but true. God can turn your sour moments into something refreshing — not just for you, but for others as well.

I once heard a teen say, *"If I hadn't gone through that, I wouldn't be able to help my friend now."* That's lemonade — God using your trials to refresh others.

"And we know that in all things God works for the good of those who love him." — Romans 8:28

Double-meaning phrase: *Lemons can become lemonade.*

Journal prompt: What's one sour experience that God might use to bless someone else?

_____

_____

_____

_____

_____

_____

_____

_____

> *Prayer: Lord, turn my struggles into a testimony*
> *that encourages others.*

WEEK 44:
COUNT IT ALL JOY

———◆◇◆———

Joy in sour seasons doesn't mean pretending everything's fine. It means trusting that God is at work, even in the midst of pain. Endurance grows best in hardship, and joy comes not from the season itself but from knowing God is in it with you.

I once heard a youth leader say, *"Joy isn't ignoring the storm; it's dancing with God in the middle of it."*

"Because you know that the testing of your faith produces perseverance." — James 1:3

Double-meaning phrase: *Joy grows in sour soil.*

Journal prompt: What's one way you can choose joy this week, even if life feels sour?

_____

_____

_____

_____

_____

_____

_____

_____

_____

Prayer: God, help me count it all joy when I face trials, knowing You are growing perseverance in me.

THE PEAR: BALANCE AND WHOLENESS

WEEK 45:
STEADY GROWTH

———◆◇◆———

A pear doesn't ripen overnight. It grows slowly, taking its time to reach sweetness. In the same way, maturity in faith isn't instant. It's steady, day by day, as you walk with Jesus.

A teacher once told a student, *"Don't rush the process — trust it."* That's peer wisdom. Growth takes patience.

"So then, just as you received Christ Jesus as Lord, continue to live your lives in him, rooted and built up in him." — Colossians 2:6 7

Double-meaning phrase: *Slow growth is still real growth.*

Journal prompt: Where in your life do you feel impatient for growth? How can you trust God's timing?

_____

_____

_____

_____

_____

_____

_____

_____

_____

> *Prayer: Lord, help me grow steady and strong in You,*
> *even if it takes time.*

WEEK 46:
BALANCED LIFE

A pear has a unique shape — wide at the bottom and narrow at the top — that is balanced and steady. God calls you to a balanced life as well: one that cares for your body, mind, relationships, and spirit. Ignore one slice, and the whole feels off.

A mentor once said, *"If you only focus on grades but ignore your soul, you'll feel empty."*

Balance matters.

"Jesus grew in wisdom and stature, and in favor with God and man." — *Luke 2:52*

Double-meaning phrase: *Balance builds strength.*

Journal prompt: Which part of your life (body, mind, spirit, relationships) feels out of balance right now?

_____

_____

_____

_____

_____

_____

Prayer: God, help me live a balanced life that honors
You in every part.

WEEK 47:
WISDOM IN RELATIONSHIPS

———◆◇◆———

Pears are often eaten with others, shared at a table. They remind us that life is healthiest when relationships are healthy. Wisdom means choosing friends wisely and investing in people who bring out the best in you.

I once overheard someone say about a teen, *"They always know how to bring peace to a group."* That's peer wisdom — adding calm instead of drama.

"Walk with the wise and become wise, for a companion of fools suffers harm." — *Proverbs 13:20*

Double-meaning phrase: *Choose pears, not poison.*

Journal prompt: Who are the friends that make you better? Who might be pulling you down?

_____

_____

_____

_____

_____

Prayer: Lord, give me wisdom to build healthy,
godly relationships.

WEEK 48:
LIVING WHOLE

———◆◇◆———

A ripe pear feels complete — soft, sweet, ready to enjoy. God wants you to live whole too, not divided or double-minded. Wholeness means integrity — being the same person at school, at home, and in private.

A youth leader once told a student, *"What makes you powerful is that you're the same person everywhere."* That's wholeness.

"I will give them an undivided heart and put a new spirit in them." — *Ezekiel 11:19*

Double-meaning phrase: *Wholeness is holiness.*

Journal prompt: Are you living one way in front of people and another way in private? How can you become whole?

> *Prayer: God, give me an undivided heart so I can live with wholeness before You and others.*

THE HARVEST

WEEK 49:
THE FRUIT OF
THE SPIRIT

———◆———

All year, you've looked at apples, bananas, grapes, and more. But the Bible names another kind of fruit — the *fruit of the Spirit*: love, joy, peace, patience, kindness, goodness, faithfulness, gentleness, and self-control.

"The fruit of the Spirit is love, joy, peace, forbearance, kindness, goodness, faithfulness, gentleness, and self-control." — Galatians 5:22-23

This fruit doesn't grow overnight. It grows as you stay close to God.

A mentor once said, *"The Spirit doesn't just change what you do; He changes who you are."* That's the fruit that lasts.

Double-meaning phrase: *Spirit fruit is the sweetest fruit.*

Journal prompt: Which fruit of the Spirit do you want to grow in most right now?

_____

_____

_____

_____

_____

_____

> *Prayer: Holy Spirit, grow Your fruit in me every day.*

WEEK 50:
SEASONS OF GROWTH

—◆◇◆—

Farmers know there's a time to plant, a time to water, and a time to harvest. Faith works the same way. You'll have seasons of waiting, seasons of growing, and seasons of breakthrough. None of them is wasted.

I once heard a teen say, *"I thought God forgot me, but later I realized He was just preparing me."* Trust the season you're in.

"There is a time for everything, and a season for every activity under the heavens." —Ecclesiastes 3:1

Double-meaning phrase: *Every season has a reason.*

Journal prompt: What season do you feel like you're in right now — planting, growing, or harvesting?

_____

_____

_____

_____

_____

_____

_____

_____

_____

> *Prayer: Lord, help me trust the season I'm in,*
> *knowing You are working in it.*

WEEK 51:
STAY ROOTED

———◆◇◆———

A tree's strength isn't seen in its branches; it's hidden in its roots. When storms come, roots decide whether the tree stands or falls. Staying rooted in Jesus means digging deep in prayer, Scripture, and worship so your faith holds steady when life shakes.

I once heard someone say, *"Storms don't grow roots; they reveal them."* What's underneath matters most.

"I am the vine; you are the branches. If you remain in me and I in you, you will bear much fruit." — John 15:5

Double-meaning phrase: *Deep roots, strong life.*

Journal prompt: What's one way you can grow deeper roots in Christ this week?

> *Prayer: God, help me stay rooted in You so I can stand firm through every storm.*

WEEK 52:
THE HARVEST

———◆◇◆———

At the end of the year, the farmer assesses the fruit harvest and the seeds planted for the future. Your life is a harvest, too. Every choice, every act of faith, every prayer is fruit that blesses others and glorifies God.

I once heard a youth pastor tell their group, *"The real goal isn't just for you to grow; it's for you to help others grow too."* That's the harvest — multiplying fruit for the kingdom.

"That person is like a tree planted by streams of water, which yields its fruit in season and whose leaf does not wither." — Psalm 1:3

Double-meaning phrase: *Fruit grows fruit.*

Journal prompt: As you look back, what fruit has God grown in you this year? What seeds will you carry into the future?

_____

_____

_____

_____

_____

_____

_____

Prayer: *Lord, thank You for the harvest of this year. Help me keep bearing fruit that lasts.*

ABOUT THE AUTHOR

D r. **Elsworth Neale** is a pastor, educator, and relationship coach passionate about equipping the next generation to live strong, faith-filled lives. With years of experience guiding teens and young adults through the challenges of identity, relationships, and purpose, Dr. Neale combines biblical truth with practical wisdom to inspire lasting transformation. He believes teenagers are not just the leaders of tomorrow—they are world changers today.

TEEN TOOLBOX

Here are a few tools to keep growing:

- **Bible Apps**: YouVersion, Bible Gateway.

- **Music**: Create worship playlists that lift your heart.

- **Community**: Join a youth group or small group. Don't do faith alone.

- **Journal**: Write down prayers, answers, struggles, and victories.